MIDDLE SCHOOL

everything you need to know
about juggling more homework,
more teachers, and more friends!

by Julie Williams
Montalbano

illustrated by
Cathi Mingus

★ American Girl®

Published by American Girl Publishing

All rights reserved. No part of this book may be used
or reproduced in any manner whatsoever without written
permission except in the case of brief quotations
embodied in critical articles and reviews.

19 20 21 22 23 24 25 QP 14 13 12 11 10 9 8 7 6 5

Editorial Development: Carrie Anton, Sara Hunt,
Darcie Johnston, Michelle Watkins
Art Direction and Design: Lisa Wilber, Chris Lorette David
Production: Jeannette Bailey, Tami Kepler, Judith Lary,
Kristi Lively, Paula Moon, Janell Wisecup

Consultants: April Moran, lower school counselor at Friends School
of Baltimore; August Frattali, principal, and Gail Womble, former principal,
at Rachel Carson Middle School in Fairfax County, Virginia

Library of Congress Cataloging-in-Publication Data
Williams, Julie.
A smart girl's guide, middle school : everything you need to know about
juggling more homework, more teachers, and more friends!
/ by Julie Williams Montalbano ; illustrated by Cathi Mingus.
pages   cm — (A smart girl's guide)
ISBN 978-1-60958-406-1 (pbk.)
1. Girls—Education (Middle school)—Handbooks, manuals, etc.—Juvenile literature.
2. Conduct of life—Juvenile literature. [1. Girls—Education (Middle school)—Handbooks,
manuals, etc.] I. Mingus, Cathi, ill. II. American girl (Middleton, Wis.) III. Title.
LC1411.W55 2014   373.236—dc23   2013025895

americangirl.com/service

Dear Reader,

Getting ready for middle school soon? Girls everywhere will be starting middle school this year—and they have a lot of the same questions that you do. Will my friends be in my classes? What if I get lost? How do I remember my locker combination?

Inside this book, you'll get the scoop on classes, homework, teachers, classrooms, and lockers. Find tips on getting organized, making new friends, and getting involved after school. Knowing what to expect in middle school makes you better prepared to handle anything that comes your way. Good luck!

Your friends at American Girl

contents

fresh start

Dear American Girl,
I'm starting middle school and I'm
completely scared. It's going to be
so different from elementary school.
How am I going to survive?

Scared

Starting middle school might feel like the scariest thing in the world to you right now. But try to think of middle school as an awesome opportunity. New teachers and new kids mean you can arrive on the first day a new you! Have you always wanted to grow out your bangs? Do you think you look more like a Katharine than a Katie? Did you ever want to learn to write poetry? Now's your chance. You can change your style, change your favorite subject, or maybe just change your attitude.

Making new friends and branching out from the same kids you've played with since kindergarten isn't such a bad thing. It's like breaking in a new pair of shoes. They might feel a little uncomfortable at first, but after a while they'll feel great!

Start with a clean slate.

how do you deal?

Middle school is all about change—new school, new teachers, new friends. How you cope with change will tell you a lot about how you'll adjust to your new surroundings. Choose the answer below that describes you best to see how you'll deal when it's for real.

1. This is the first year you have to take the bus to and from school. When you find this out, you . . .

   a. beg your dad to ask his boss to let him leave early every day to pick you up.

   b. call around to see if any other friends will be on your bus. Maybe you can sit together.

2. When your favorite teacher goes on maternity leave and is replaced with a substitute for the rest of the school year, you . . .

   a. find yourself saying, "That's not how Ms. Cho did it."

   b. help bring the new teacher up to speed on where Ms. Cho left off, and then let her do her own thing.

3. When you find out that none of your friends are in your classes this year, you . . .

   a. ask the guidance counselor to change your schedule so that you can be with your friends.

   b. feel bummed, but talk yourself into braving it alone.

4. Your brother says you'll have only three minutes to get from one class to another in middle school. You . . .

   a. gasp, "No way! I'll never make it."

   b. set a timer for three minutes to see just how long you'll have between classes.

5. Your best friend starts hanging out with a new girl at school. You . . .

   a. get jealous and give your friend the cold shoulder, hoping she'll get the hint that you don't like what she's doing.

   b. try to get to know the new girl. Maybe she'll turn out to be a great friend for you, too!

6. Your soccer coach scratches you from the starting lineup. You . . .

   a. sulk over to the bench and decide that soccer isn't your thing.

   b. stay on the sidelines and cheer the team on. If you pick up some good tips from the game, you might be able to earn back your position.

If you answered

Mostly a's
You're a holdout.
When change happens to you, you try to hang on to the way things used to be. Why? Because you know what to expect and what to do. You feel in control. But now that something new has come along, you're afraid you've lost control. **Don't be so quick to run.** New faces, places, and challenges can open up a whole new world for you. **And there is something you'll always have control over: how you handle and react to things.** As the unknown becomes more familiar, you'll find yourself feeling more sure of yourself.

Mostly b's
You like to go with the flow.
When faced with a big change, you take a deep breath and do your best. You know that nothing ever stays the same, and it's up to you to make the most of what's to come. Since you'll be making more of your own decisions in middle school, **it's important to keep your wits about you.** You'll have more responsibility and learn to manage more things on your own, which can make you feel really grown-up and make your parents proud of you.

Picture yourself having a good time in middle school.

Positive visualization is a trick that professional athletes use all the time. If you want to do well in a given situation, you have to want it, feel it, see it. That's not to say that you can close your eyes and imagine success one time and it will come. But it's a start! If you tell yourself you can do something, you've taken the first step toward making it a reality.

rise 'n' shine

In your school district, the middle-school day might start earlier than the elementary-school day. Maybe you walked to school before, but now you ride the bus. Or you might have a lot more after-school activities this year. How you start your day will set the pace for your super-busy middle-school schedule. Do you start your day sunny-side up or in a scramble? Which description sounds most like you?

Sunny-side up

You're up and out of bed as soon as the alarm sounds. Hey, you even have time to look over your homework before hitting the road. Keep on rising and shining!

Over easy

You like to ease yourself awake with a couple of swipes at the snooze button. You have a special ability to know when to rest and when to rise—often getting out of bed at the very last possible minute. But if you find yourself slipping back to sleep more and more often each morning, consider putting that alarm clock across the room.

Scrambled

Dream visions cloud your head as you rush out the door. A morning meal is nothing but a blur—if you had time to sit down to breakfast at all. You're frazzled and stressed out even before you get to school. What's the problem? You're not giving yourself enough time to get ready. Try getting up 15 minutes earlier. You'll be surprised how much easier the morning will be when you give yourself a couple extra minutes to gather your thoughts before heading out for the day.

FACT: On average, 11-year-old girls need ten hours of sleep each night. That means if you have to get up at 6:00 a.m., you should try to be in bed by 8:00 p.m.

WHAT?!

Not going to happen? It's probably been years since you went to bed at 8:00 p.m. But it's at least reason to rethink that 10:00 p.m. bedtime you're trying to negotiate.

"what do I wear?"

A well-organized wardrobe can make a big difference when you're getting ready for school in a hurry. Follow these tips to get out the door feeling dressed for success.

★ **Clean clothes.** Make sure you have five or six outfits that you like to wear. That way, you'll have to do laundry just once a week and you'll have something clean for each day of the school week.

★ **Mix & match separates.** Buying clothes in basic colors makes it easier to create lots of different outfits. Make your style your own by adding jewelry, hair thingies, and other accessories.

★ **Clean out your closet.** Get rid of clothes that are too small by donating them to charity.

★ **Layers.** Layers allow you to adjust to the temperature throughout the day. You can tie a sweatshirt around your waist if you get warm.

★ **A clock.** A must-have for every middle schooler is a way to keep track of time, whether it's on your electronic device or on your wrist.

★ **Comfy shoes.** You need one pair for school and one for gym. Also have a pair in your closet for dressing up for the band concert.

★ **Crack the code.** Check your school's dress code and make sure the clothes you plan to wear are appropriate.

getting there

What if I oversleep and get to school late? Will I get into big trouble?

Sleepy Samara

If you know you're going to be late, ask your mom or dad to write a note or call the school explaining why. It's OK to be tardy once in a while if you have a good reason. By middle school, though, you're expected to be there before the bell rings. If oversleeping is a problem for you, this is a good time to start working on new habits.

Last school year, I was late almost every day. Next year I am going to middle school, and I'll have to get up even earlier. I need a plan to help me get ready in the morning. Help!

Not OK

Take a look at your morning schedule and see where you can gain some time. Do you need to set the alarm to go off earlier? Or maybe you should talk to your siblings about letting you in the bathroom first. Try some of the organization tips on the next page to get yourself up and out in the morning.

get into the habit

Make busy school days a bit easier by sticking to a **basic routine.**
Doing tasks in the same order each day will help you remember what
needs to be done. After a while, you'll whip through your routine in
no time.

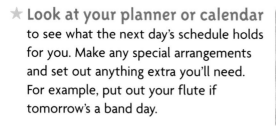

The night before

★ **Look at your planner or calendar**
to see what the next day's schedule holds
for you. Make any special arrangements
and set out anything extra you'll need.
For example, put out your flute if
tomorrow's a band day.

★ Set out or at least **think about what you're going to wear**
the next day. Is your outfit clean?

★ **Pack your backpack** or book
bag so that you can just grab it and
go in the morning. **Homework
done?**

★ Ask Mom or Dad to **sign any papers** or write any notes you
need for the next day.

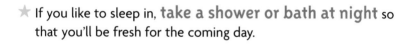

★ Pack your lunch or, if you need it,
tuck **lunch money** into your
backpack or book bag.

★ If you like to sleep in, **take a shower or bath at night** so
that you'll be fresh for the coming day.

★ **Tuck in with a good book** to help you relax and get into
dream mode.

The morning rush hour

★ **Stretch!**

★ Bathe or shower if you didn't the night before. If you did, just **freshen up quickly** in the bathroom.

★ **Get dressed.**

★ **Eat breakfast—** preferably sitting down!

★ Do a **quick mirror check** to make sure your hair is neat and your shirt isn't inside out.

★ **Grab** your stuff **and go.**

Breakfast Bets

Everyone knows it's really important to have breakfast every morning. But did you know that the wrong kind of breakfast can leave you tired and sluggish around mid-morning? Foods high in processed sugars and flour, such as sweetened cereals and frosted toaster pastries, can actually zap your energy. Instead, try to eat whole-grain foods, fruits, and protein to keep you going. Some good choices are whole-wheat toast with peanut butter, granola, an apple or banana, yogurt, oatmeal, or a glass of milk.

before you go

Even more important than school supplies and new shoes is bringing a good attitude with you as you head to middle school.

Be self-confident.

Almost every girl cares what other people think about her—especially when meeting new classmates or trying out a new look. **It's natural to be a little unsure of yourself** in new situations, but try not to think the worst when things are left unsaid. If someone is staring at your new haircut, she may be thinking how it would look on her!

Be realistic.

You skipped over question #3 on the test and blew your chance for a perfect score. So you spend the rest of the day thinking: *How could I be so stupid?* **Give yourself a break.** Don't beat yourself up over every little mistake. Instead, celebrate what you did right, and accept and understand what you did wrong. Then move on, knowing that you did the best you could do.

Be levelheaded.

Worrying sucks up your energy. Don't let thoughts about what could go wrong eat away at your precious time, or you'll be left with nothing to show for it—except a bellyful of butterflies. Focus on what good things could happen: *I might get an A!* If you have to consider the negative "what-ifs," follow up each one with a positive "what-if." Give yourself five minutes; then **get on with things.**

Be open-minded.

Much of your time in middle school is spent getting tested, graded, and evaluated. Teacher comments, class critics, and even input from parents can sometimes hurt. Try to take each comment one at a time and see if you can use the advice that's given. **Don't take it personally or get discouraged.** Remind yourself:

> I'm a good person.
> My math skills just
> need a little work.

Don't worry—you'll be just fine. Soon enough, **YOU** could be giving advice to someone else who is scared about starting middle school, just like you were.

new school

Dear American Girl,
I'm going to middle school next year, but I'm not sure I'm ready for all the responsibility yet. What if I forget which classroom to go to, or if I get to class late and get detention?

Kate

As soon as you get your schedule and a school map, locate each of your classrooms on the map and trace the route you'll take from room to room. Then make sure you stash your map in your backpack or tape it inside your locker.

If you have the opportunity to "walk through" your schedule before the first day of school, by all means do it! If your school doesn't allow this, it's not a big deal. No one will expect you to know your way around right away.

What to look for:

- ★ your locker
- ★ your homeroom
- ★ your classrooms
- ★ girls' bathrooms
- ★ cafeteria (lunchroom)
- ★ nurse's office
- ★ counselor's office
- ★ main office
- ★ gym and locker room
- ★ drinking fountains

getting around

Chances are, your middle school will be bigger than your elementary school. Just think of it as room to grow. You'll be navigating the halls like a pro in no time.

Lost and found

★ **Classroom numbers** typically start with the number of the floor they are on. For example, room 101 is on the first floor and room 201 is on the second floor.

★ **Drinking fountains** are almost always located near the bathrooms.

★ **Stairways** are usually at the ends of halls. Look for exit signs.

★ **Use visual landmarks** to help remember which way to go. "Take a left at the trophy case, pass the room with the hamsters . . ."

One way

Hallways can get pretty crowded between classes. Try to stick to your right to stay with the flow of traffic—like on a freeway!

Afraid you'll be late?

Don't panic. Just walk as quickly as you can. Don't stop to talk—instead, ask your friend to walk with you as you chat. Plan a stop at your locker only when it's on your way. That means that you might have to carry more than one class's books with you at a time. If you need more time than is allowed between classes to go to the bathroom or pick up something at the office, ask a teacher for permission or a hall pass.

Home sweet homeroom

You may be assigned to go to a room first thing every morning and at the end of every day. There your homeroom teacher will take attendance and you'll listen to announcements. When the bell rings, it's off to your first class!

In some middle schools, you might not switch for every class during the first year you're there. Instead, you'll have a homeroom teacher for your core classes, much like you did in elementary school. If your district does this, you'll have even more time to adjust to the changes.

Ding-a-ling!

Bells may sound to signal the beginning and end of class. You may also hear a "tardy" bell before a final bell to let you know you have one minute or so to get into your seat before you're counted late.

your locker

You'll be assigned a numbered locker to store your coat, books, and school supplies. Your locker may seem hard to find at first because there are rows upon rows of identical lockers. Just look for the number, use a landmark such as a nearby drinking fountain or class-room, or count down from the end of the row. Once you've visited your locker a few times, you'll know right where to go.

I'll have a locker for the first time this year. What if I can't open it or I forget the combination to the lock?

Locked Out

Either your locker will come with a built-in combination lock or you'll be asked to bring your own padlock. Usually the combination is a set of three numbers. All you need to do is turn the dial to those numbers in a certain order. Here's how most locks work:

1. Turn the dial to the right two full turns, and line up the first number of the combination with the notch at the top of the lock. You may feel a little tightness or hear a slight click when you do this.

2. Turn the dial to the left, pass the first number once, and line up the second number with the notch.

3. Turn the dial back to the right and line up the third number with the notch. Lift the handle or pull down on the padlock to open. Success!

4. To close, keep the third number lined up with the notch, and push the bar back into the lock. Spin the dial to set the lock.

Just remember **"right, left, right."** With a little practice, you'll master the combination and have time to spare before your next class.

It's a good idea to **write down the combination and keep it in a secret place,** such as inside a folder or your assignment book, until you know it by heart. If you have trouble opening the locker for any reason, go to your next class and deal with it later. Your homeroom teacher, or someone in the main office or guidance area, should be able to help you during lunch or after school.

Don't share your locker combination with anyone. Treat it like a key to your house—you wouldn't want the whole school to have that, would you?

I memorized my combination before school even started. I just practiced over and over again at home.

moving in

You got the list of supplies from your school. Here's some stuff that wasn't on the list.

★ Hang an organizer inside your locker to stash extra pencils, sticky notes, and even batteries for your calculator. Look for an organizer that has a mirror and a place to keep a brush or comb.

★ Keep a "just-in-case kit" in your organizer with hair elastics, tissues, safety pins, bandages, tampons or pads, and change for vending machines.

What not to keep in your locker:

★ food or drinks (except in a lunch bag)

★ more than $5 in cash

★ expensive jewelry and gadgets and other treasured, valuable, or irreplaceable things that could get stolen

★ sweaty gym clothes and sneakers (ewww!)

Once a week, clean out the papers in your locker. File them, recycle them, or take them home. **NOTE:** Check school rules before hanging anything in your locker. Also talk to a locker mate, if you have one, before doing any major interior design.

pack perfect

I just started middle school, and my backpack weighs 20 pounds! My shoulders and back are always sore. What can I do to lighten my load?

Backpack Blues

Here are some tips for carrying the weight of middle school on your shoulders.

★ Carry your backpack over both shoulders, not just one. Otherwise, your pack may become a *real* pain in the neck.

★ Use a pack with padded shoulder straps.

★ Don't try to carry everything you need for the whole day. Park some books in your locker until you need them.

★ Put heavier, bigger books closer to your back.

★ Don't hang key chains or doodads off the zippers. They can get caught on something and stop you in your tracks.

★ Consider a rolling bag for extra-heavy baggage days.

★ Keep your pack neat by cleaning it out twice a week.

★ If you have a messenger bag, carry it with the strap across your body so that the weight gets distributed more evenly.

take a seat

If where to sit is up to you, think before you choose. Some seats make learning easier, while others make it harder for you to focus on your work.

If you're next to the pencil sharpener, you may find yourself chatting with everyone who stops to use it. The noise can be distracting during tests, too.

A seat by the door will get you in and out of the room quickly, but you may also find yourself waving to anyone who walks by.

It's easy to get lost back here. If you find yourself stuck in the boonies, let the teacher know if you can't hear what she's saying or see what she's writing on the board.

Sit by someone you'd like to know better.

Caution! Window seats can be distracting!

Don't be afraid to sit near the teacher's desk.

Sit in the center rows, where you're more likely to stay in the thick of things.

teachers

Dear American Girl,
I'm going into sixth grade and to a new school. I'm scared because there will be new teachers! I've heard bad rumors about them. What should I do?
Scaredy Cat

You might be surprised to learn that middle-school teachers are a whole lot like your elementary-school teachers. The difference is that they chose to teach middle school because they enjoy working with kids your age.

Five Facts About Middle School Teachers

1. They have a lot of students. It's up to you to make sure you get the help you need.

2. They can make mistakes. Go easy on them if they do.

3. Nothing's more frustrating to a teacher than having to spend precious class time disciplining unruly kids. Be respectful and try not to get caught up in any distracting classroom antics.

4. They want to know what you think. Pick the right time to tell them.

5. They want to help you do well. That's their job.

teacher types

In elementary school you might have spent all day with just one or two teachers, and you became very close to them. Now you could have a different teacher for every class. You'll want to get to know each one and adjust to each individual teaching style.

Ms. Mom

Quote: "Repeat after me."

Style: Teaches by example. Shows students how to do things rather than just telling them.

Pros: Gives frequent praise. Welcomes any contribution, whether it's significant or not.

Cons: Doesn't hide her feelings when someone lets her down by forgetting homework or doing poorly on a test.

Warning: You may feel babied.

Don't: Take advantage of her chumminess. She'll be The Boss if you force her to be.

Do: Keep your eyes open because you'll be expected to learn by observing. Do the best you can, and be happy with the results—even if they aren't exactly the same as the teacher's.

The Boss

Quote: "Listen up!"

Style: Clearly explains lessons and the way to do things. Gives both positive and negative feedback. Relays info through class lectures. Follows the lesson plan closely.

Pros: You know exactly what's expected of you.

Cons: Doesn't allow much class discussion.

Warning: He may seem unapproachable.

Don't: Assume he doesn't like you or is mean.

Do: Follow the rules he sets. If you find yourself a bit scared of this teacher, remember that he's there to help you. The more you talk to him, the easier it will be to understand his approach and expectations.

Speed Racer

Quote: "Try to stay with me."

Style: Smart. Knows her subject inside and out. Moves through lessons quickly. Gives a lot of challenging assignments.

Pros: Pushes you to do your best.

Cons: May cover material too quickly. May not take the time to fully explain the reasons for an answer. Tends to give a lot of work.

Warning: You may get left in the dust.

Don't: Get frustrated and think that you're so lost or so far behind that you just give up trying.

Do: Raise your hand and ask the teacher to repeat the information if you miss an important point. Chances are, you weren't the only one who didn't get it. If you fall behind, catch up as soon as you can.

Freestyle

Quote: "Let's break into groups."

Style: Loves to brainstorm. Teaches by asking questions and fielding answers from the class. Explores different ways of learning and doing things.

Pros: Lets students work on their own. Gives lots of feedback and support.

Cons: Letting everyone have a say can eat up class time, leaving some material uncovered.

Warning: You may not get a clear idea of what's "right" and what's "wrong." Some students get anxious when they are given too much independence.

Don't: Clam up and keep your thoughts to yourself.

Do: Share your opinions and be open to those of others. Don't be afraid to ask the teacher to make an assignment more clear or ask for more direction.

first impressions

Regardless of your teacher's style, you'll want to do your best to get the most out of each class.

Pay attention

Keep your eyes wide open. Watch what's going up on the board, where your teacher is pointing, or how a classmate's experiment looks. Make eye contact with your teacher when you speak to her and when she's talking to the class. This will let her know that you're interested in what she has to say.

Listen up

Lend an ear to classroom discussions, lectures, and announcements. If you don't understand something, don't be quick to cut the teacher off with a question. See if he answers your question in his next couple of sentences. If not, go ahead and raise your hand.

Speak up

Ask questions about anything you don't understand. Offer answers when the teacher asks questions. Take part in discussions by saying what you think about a topic. Class participation can make or break your final grade. But think before you speak. Asking too many not-well-thought-out questions could tell your teacher that you weren't listening.

Hands on

Take notes to help the info sink in and to refresh your memory later. Practice using math formulas on the board. Try your hand at an experiment. The time will seem to go by faster, and your teacher will note your enthusiasm.

Stay tuned . . . even when you're not in school.

★ Keep up with current events by bookmarking your favorite online news sites and visiting them regularly.

★ Challenge yourself with crosswords, brainteasers, trivia games, even jigsaw puzzles.

★ Compare prices at the grocery store.

★ Make up radio commercials for businesses near your house.

★ On the road, figure out how long it will take to get where you're going—divide miles to go by the speed limit.

★ Plant something and watch it grow.

got a question?

I'm having trouble in math. How can I ask for help without feeling stupid?

Math Meltdown

Asking for help isn't stupid—it's smart. You're taking responsibility for what you learn. Teachers and parents will be very happy about that. And it's no secret that the students who get better grades are often the ones who ask the most questions.

A good way to ask for help is to talk to your teacher before or after class so that the pressure of doing it in front of your classmates is off. Let her know what you're having trouble with. Be specific. Then ask your teacher when would be a good time to sit down and work through your problem together. You'll want to make sure you have enough time to clear up all your questions. Say something like, "I need help with positive and negative integers. Can you help me work through a couple of problems after school one day?"

"Ask me."

Teachers may be your first line of assistance in class, but they are most definitely not the only resource you have. Depending on what confuses you, you can call on any number of helpers in middle school (and beyond!):

- ★ friends
- ★ online resources
- ★ Mom/Dad
- ★ a librarian
- ★ a tutor
- ★ older siblings
- ★ classmates
- ★ a school counselor

When you are having trouble in a class, tell your parents. It might be hard to go to your parents with an "I need help," but do it anyway. They're on your side.

How to Make the Most of the Help You Get

1. Listen. Don't interrupt the explanation. Let your helper talk you through the answer.

2. Take notes.

3. Repeat back to your helper what she said to make sure you got it right.

4. Ask if you can work through a problem together. That may help pinpoint exactly where you're getting stuck.

5. Don't be afraid to tell your helper that you still don't understand. She'll try to explain a different way.

6. Try solving the problem on your own.

teacher troubles

I just started the sixth grade. I was getting very good grades, but now I'm starting to get bad grades. I want to show them to my parents, but I'm afraid I'll let them down or they will be mad. Please help!

Worried

In middle school, you'll have increased demands on your time. You'll have more responsibility than ever before, and your teachers will expect a whole lot more from you, so you may experience a temporary fall in grades. Once you adjust to the more rigorous schedule and expectations, you should be able to get back to your true form.

However, falling grades could be a sign that you're being asked to learn or perform in a different way than you did in elementary school. Talk with a guidance counselor and your teachers to find out what new skills you need to develop to succeed in middle school.

I've heard that my middle-school teachers give out detentions. I'm nervous and afraid I'll get one. What happens there?

Dreading Detention

Depending on your school, detention may mean having to stay after school and help a teacher, sit in a classroom and think about what you've done, or write an essay explaining why what you did was wrong. Many students are allowed to do homework or read during detention. If you get a detention, find out what's expected of you, and show up prepared to serve your time. And don't forget to arrange for a ride home when it's over.

I have a new teacher who yells and jumps if you get something wrong. I don't want to be yelled at. What can I do?

Help!

Teachers who are very serious about their subjects may do just about anything to motivate their students to do better in class. Your teacher probably learned over the years that jumping and yelling get attention. Try to listen to what she says, not how loudly she yells. Once you adjust to her style, you may learn to appreciate—or at least understand—her intensity.

My chorus teacher seems to not like me, but I love to sing, so I don't want to quit. What can I do to make third period more enjoyable?

Voice of Reason

Sometimes a student and a teacher just don't click, but that doesn't mean you can't get what you need out of class. Is there something you do that your teacher doesn't respond well to? For example, do you giggle between songs or come to class unprepared? If so, change the way you behave in the class to see if it makes a difference. Is he nice to other kids in the class? Pay attention to what they do or say that he seems to like. If it's something you can improve on, try it. But it could simply be that he prefers to keep a more professional line drawn between teacher and student. If so, don't let that stop you from learning more about music. He probably has a lot to share.

subject matters

Dear American Girl,
This year I'm going to be switching classes.
I don't know if I'll be able to handle homework
from so many different teachers along with all
of the things I have to do after school.
Too Much to Do?

It's the moment you've been waiting for—you finally get your class schedule. While you'll recognize many of the same subjects from elementary school, some classes might be new to you, such as Family and Consumer Education, Technology, Foreign Language, or Health.

Though change can make you nervous, in middle school you'll likely have variety not just in what you're learning, but in how and when you learn, too.

Your schedule might rotate (meaning classes aren't in the same order every day), and some classes may alternate (meaning you have one class one day and a different class the next). But that's what keeps things interesting.

It's true that you'll probably have more homework. But you may quickly find that the more you have to do, the more you're able to get done!

class notes

The Basics

English

In middle school, the stages of writing—brainstorming, drafting, editing, and revising—will become more important as you create bigger and better reports.

Smart Girl's Tip: Think while you read. Get more out of reading assignments by asking yourself questions like "What's the main point of this story?" or "What makes this character do what she does?"

Math

You'll use the same basic math skills in middle school that you learned in elementary school to solve more challenging problems and equations. Word problems will become more complex, and you'll learn how to solve for the unknown in beginning algebra.

Smart Girl's Tip: Most of the math you'll do in middle school builds on skills you've already learned. Brush up on the basics before school starts!

Social Studies

This year you'll be assigned a lot of hands-on projects. You'll learn about ancient civilizations and discover history right in your own backyard as you explore your state's history.

Smart Girl's Tip: You may also spend some time each week talking about current events, so keep up with the world around you by watching or reading the news regularly.

Science

You'll get to do more experiments and lab work this year as you explore chemical reactions and microorganisms. And you'll never look at a rock the same way after learning about fossils, natural resources, and the environment.

Smart Girl's Tip: Just because an experiment fails doesn't mean *you* have failed. What counts is that you record your results accurately. Be patient and honest when performing experiments, and take good notes!

Gym/Health

For many girls, middle school is the first time that they find they have to change clothes in front of others. To ease your anxiety, remember that everyone feels self-conscious. Showers are usually optional (though you might want to take one!). Many schools alternate gym and health classes. In health, you'll learn about the human body and will likely separate into boys-only and girls-only groups for some personal discussions.

Smart Girl's Tip: Pack baby wipes or hand wipes into your gym bag to freshen up with after class. Keep barrettes, hair elastics, or a headband handy for quick hair fixes.

Chart Your Course

To learn more about the different classes, ask your new school for a course description book or check the school's website for a "curriculum" link. And feel free to ask teachers or older students any questions that you may have. Don't create your schedule based on what your friends are taking. Pick the courses that interest you most.

Electives

Beyond the basics, you'll get to choose one or two other courses to take. Here are a few notes about the elective classes your school may offer:

Foreign Languages

Many middle schools offer classes in Spanish, French, German, Latin, even Japanese. If you can't decide which language to take, think about which culture is most interesting to you or which language you might use the most.

Smart Girl's Tip: You'll probably have to commit to one foreign language in high school. If your school allows it, use your time in middle school to sample a few different languages that interest you before settling on one.

Band or Orchestra

Learn how to play an instrument and read music. Many schools have their own instruments that they loan to students. Others require that you rent or buy your own instrument. You might compete for a seat and get to perform onstage at concerts.

Smart Girl's Tip: When deciding what instrument is right for you, think about the types of sounds you're drawn to. Find out from the band or orchestra director which instrument needs more players. If playing an instrument isn't your thing but you enjoy music, many schools offer chorus, too.

Art

In middle school, you'll be taught drawing, painting, and sculpting techniques. You'll also have more sophisticated materials to work with and more freedom to explore your creativity.

Smart Girl's Tip: In addition to being fun, the time you spend in art will help you develop skills you need to solve problems in other subjects.

Home Economics/Family and Consumer Education

Here you'll learn basic life skills, such as how to balance a checkbook, create and stick to a budget, sew yourself something snazzy, take care of little kids, and create great meals. You'll also begin to explore careers that you might like when you get older.

Smart Girl's Tip: Practice your new skills at home, and your parents will be pleased!

Free Period/Study Hall

Many middle schools assign students a free period once a day or a few times a week. Free periods last as long as a regular class and often take the place of those recesses you had in elementary school. What you do with this block of time is up to you—as long as you're quiet. Get a head start on homework, research an upcoming paper, or study for a quiz.

Smart Girl's Tip: Free periods are great for busy students who don't have a lot of time after school for homework.

Computers and Technology

In this class, you'll learn basic programming skills and get hands-on experience using word processing, spreadsheet, and database programs. You'll also learn about conducting online and database searches for research reports. And you may have the opportunity to try your hand at designing or managing a website.

Smart Girl's Tip: Whether you're searching online for homework help, preparing a presentation, designing a book report, or building a website, computers can help you make the grade—that is, if you know how to make them work for you.

keep it together

You'll have a lot more papers—from handouts to homework—to shuffle in middle school. Establish your own system for storing (and weeding out!) those papers. The sooner you can find what you're looking for, the sooner you can get your work done.

Code it

Color-code your notebooks, folders, and binder tabs— red for math, blue for science, and so on. Keep a folder for general school papers, too, such as permission slips, lunch menus, and the like.

Store it

You're likely to lose or mangle loose papers if you stuff them into a textbook or throw them into your backpack or locker—not to mention that you'll never be able to find an important paper when you need it. So take an extra second to slip any loose papers that you get into their subject folders or binders.

Paper trail

Keep homework assignments, papers, quizzes, and tests for at least a month to review for tests, track your grade, or prove that you did them. Take papers home and store them in magazine files (available at office-supply stores) or binders labeled for each subject. At the end of each grading period, go through the files and recycle what you no longer need.

On Your Own

Because middle-school teachers have many more students to teach, they won't be able to keep as close a watch over your work as you were used to in elementary school. It's not that they don't care. Rather, they trust you to follow through on what's asked. Use what you learned in elementary school to solve problems or determine what the next step should be on your own.

If you miss school for more than two days, send your homework assignments to your teachers through a neighbor or sibling. Also, it's a good idea to write notes to your teachers explaining what homework you did or didn't understand. This shows your teachers that you are responsible.

"why do I have so much homework?"

Homework may seem like a random attempt by teachers to occupy all your free time. But there's definitely a method to the homework madness. Middle-school teachers assign three basic types of homework. If you know *why* you're doing it, it might seem more worth your while.

1. Preparation homework

Teachers assign reading, library or online research, or collecting examples such as news articles to get you ready for the next day's class discussion. While you're doing this work, flag anything that may need a little more explanation or jot down questions to ask the teacher in class. Getting this homework done is key to participating in class and staying on top of things—especially if you're graded on class participation.

2. Practice homework

Once you've been introduced to a new subject or concept, teachers assign tasks so that you can practice what you've learned—from diagramming sentences to solving equations. The more you practice, the better you'll understand.

3. Performance homework

After you've had a chance to practice, teachers will ask you to *perform*, or show how well you understand a topic. Studying for a test, writing a paper, and presenting a group report are good examples of this type of assignment. If you're prepared and you've practiced, you'll be ready to perform.

Time It Right

If you like to get the pencil scratching out of the way first, do your "practice" work first thing when you get home from school. Then soak up the reading assignment closer to bedtime, when things are more relaxed and quiet. Match your mood or your energy level to your work, and you'll find that homework becomes less of a chore and more of a routine.

get it done

With six or seven teachers assigning homework instead of just one, you may get slammed some nights. Try not to whine about it.

Be prepared to sit for a spell. Grab a snack and a glass of water to keep nearby so that you won't have an excuse to get up and wander into the kitchen.

The best way to fight the temptation to watch TV is to leave it off until you've finished your homework. Likewise, save time eaters such as texting and online games for after you're done with homework.

Some more tips to succeeding in class:

Write neatly.

Proofread your work.

Hand in work on time.

Make your first effort your best
(no more re-dos).

If you do your
homework,
you'll do
better
in school.

excuses, excuses

> But it's so boring!

If you get an assignment that's a big snore, find a way to make it more interesting. Pretend you're a contestant on a history game show. Imagine you're an actress trying out for a part in your English assignment. There are lots of ways to breathe life into the subject you're studying. Use your imagination and turn your work into play.

Smart Girl's Tip: If sitting still for extended periods makes you wiggle, take breaks every half hour or so to keep your head in the game.

> I didn't have time to finish it all.

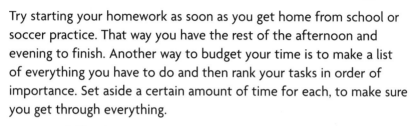

Try starting your homework as soon as you get home from school or soccer practice. That way you have the rest of the afternoon and evening to finish. Another way to budget your time is to make a list of everything you have to do and then rank your tasks in order of importance. Set aside a certain amount of time for each, to make sure you get through everything.

Smart Girl's Tip: Chip away at long-term assignments—do a little every night, since you never know what you'll be assigned right before the big project is due.

I forgot.

Before you leave school at the end of the day, look over your "to do" list and think about what you'll need to get done before tomorrow. To help, put books you have to take home in your backpack throughout the day. When the final bell rings, just get anything you need for your last class, grab your pack, and you're off!

Smart Girl's Tip: Create a contact list with the name of at least one person in every class. When you have a question about an assignment, you can call your study buddy. If you're reading a book at school and need to bring it home for assigned reading or homework, try getting a second copy from the local library. Keep one at home, and leave one at school. Brilliant!

Things were too noisy at home last night.

If you have too many distractions at home, pack up and head to where you can focus better. Try the library, the backyard, even Grandma's place. If you have to stick around the house, choose the quietest room for doing your homework and call it your Homework Zone. Let others know that you need to be left alone.

Smart Girl's Tip: If you're easily distracted by clutter and movement around you, try working alone in a clean room.

I forgot my book.

Keep a running "to do" list throughout the day, and don't forget to look at it. Check things off as you complete them. You'd be surprised how many things you overlook or neglect because you thought you could remember what you needed to do and didn't write it down.

Smart Girl's Tip: At the beginning of each day, review your "to do" list from the day before. If anything's still left undone, put it on the top of today's list.

test time

Whenever I have a really big test coming up, I study so hard for it. Then, while I'm taking the test, I completely blank out! What should I do?!

Blank Out in Maryland

Blanking out can be a sign of overactive nerves. You've gotten yourself so worked up about what could go wrong that when the time comes to show your stuff, you freeze. Balance your thoughts of impending doom with images of success. Take a moment at the start of a test to take a deep breath and calm down.

Be ready to write

In middle school you'll be asked to answer more essay questions on your tests. Be prepared to write about:

★ Steps to processes—list the order in which something happens.

★ Pros and cons—weigh the good against the bad.

★ Reasons for and against—present both sides of an argument.

★ Compare and contrast—discuss how two things are alike and different.

★ Causes and effects—describe how something came about and what happened when it did.

Test-Taking Tutorial

Make sure your pencil is sharp or your pen's ink is flowing well. When you get the test, read the instructions and do a quick scan of the whole thing—just so you know how long the test is. This will help you manage your time better. Will you need to write an essay at the end? Allow enough time for that. But don't rush either.

★ Take a deep breath and dig in.

★ Think before you write an answer.

★ It's not a race. Take a mini break every now and then. Stretch your fingers if you find they're getting crampy. Roll your neck.

★ If you don't know an answer, guess. Don't leave any questions blank.

★ Look over your answers before turning in your paper. Make sure you didn't miss any questions or leave important facts out of an essay.

★ If a question asks for four reasons, count to make sure you've mentioned all of them.

★ Take a stab at any extra-credit questions.

Absolutely, positively make sure your name is on your paper.

making the grade

In elementary school, your grades might have depended not only on what you did but also on how hard you tried. In middle school, your grades will become more about performance and less about effort.

What makes up my grade?

Every homework assignment, class discussion, quiz, paper, and test will be rated and rolled together to get the grade that goes onto your report card.

Here are the kinds of tasks and skills you might be scored on:

★ Just about all teachers use tests and quizzes to determine how well you remember information that's been presented in class or your ability to solve problems.

★ Each homework assignment will be graded. Late—or worse, missing—work can really hurt your final grade. Neatness usually counts.

★ Some teachers might ask you to recite information that you've memorized—the faster, the better! But accuracy is key for drills.

★ Papers, projects, and presentation grades are based on your planning, performance, and problem-solving skills while working on the project, as well as the end result.

★ Your willingness to offer comments, ask and answer questions, or just generally be on the ball during class will determine your level of class participation.

★ In some classes, you might be asked to turn in your notebook for the teacher to grade. Yep! Even the neatness and completeness of your note taking could be up for review.

★ When a teacher is assessing your organization skills, she might consider how well you use that trusty assignment book to keep a running list of your weekly workload.

Different teachers rank each area differently. At the beginning of the year, ask each of your teachers how she plans to come up with her final grades.

Grade Grief

The book report you worked on all last week comes back with red marks all over it. Ouch! Here's how to handle it.

Don't take it too personally.
Just because your teacher had some tough comments about your paper doesn't mean he hates you. In fact, he wants you to do better, knows you can do better, and is showing you how you can do better.

Be honest with yourself.
Could you have done better? Take a look at each comment. Did you make a silly mistake? Did you miss the point? Take responsibility for your work. Ask for suggestions on how to improve if you need them.

Take the bad and make it good.
Those comments on your paper let you know exactly what the teacher expects of you next time. Use them as a checklist when you get ready to write your next report.

"whadja get?"

My friends always ask me what I got on my tests. Sometimes I don't want to tell them, but how do I avoid it without looking like a dork?

No Dork

Keeping your grade to yourself is tricky because, in a way, you're creating a secret. And you know what some kids do when they know you have a secret: They imagine all sorts of things that aren't true. "Did she fail?" "What's the big deal about sharing?" But you can prevent rumors from starting by saying no the right way. You're not hiding anything; you're just not offering anything, either. When asked to reveal your grade, say something like, "If you don't mind, I'd prefer to keep it to myself." Or try to avoid the question ("I'm sure you did really well. That's great!") or change the subject altogether ("Hey, are you going to the dance on Friday?").

Every girl wants to know where she stands in the class. Grades are the most visible measure. In middle school, the pressure to be on top can be stronger than ever before. Keep the competition you're involved in healthy, not stressful.

Friendly competition

Competing with other classmates for the best grade isn't all bad. Wanting to do as well as or better than they do can fuel your studying or push you to go the extra mile on your report. In fact, you probably like to study with several different close friends. One of the reasons you're friends is because you admire each other's abilities. You coach each other to do the best that you can.

Grade raid

You got a B and your best friend got an A. This can be a real bummer. When you play the grade game, naturally you want to win. But when you lose, you're sore. Don't make your wounds worse by coming up with silly excuses, blaming the teacher, being jealous of your friend, or being too hard on yourself. Instead, look over your paper to find out where your weaknesses were, and then promise yourself that you'll do better next time.

Cutthroat competition

The urge to get a better score than everyone else can get ugly. If you get caught up in the race, you may waste precious study time worrying about how you'll measure up. You may even secretly wish for friends to do poorly. Don't even go there. Instead, focus on competing with yourself. Try to maintain your good grades or do better than your last score—not your friend's.

to cheat or not to cheat?

That is the question.

But if we all know the answer, why are some girls still tempted?

"Everyone else is doing it."

When "everyone else" seems to be cheating, it's oh-so-easy to slip into the quicksand. Why should you risk getting a B when everyone else is sure to get an A? Before you go over to the dark side, think about this: cheating is wrong. Not to mention the answers you're copying could be wrong. But even if they are right, what will the teacher think when everyone gets the same score? Teachers are smarter than you think. You'll be smarter than the others when you go your own way and learn the material. And when the teacher starts a new lesson that builds on the one you were just tested on, you'll be up to speed while the others fall behind.

"I can't say no to my friend."

Why is it so hard to say no when a friend asks to copy your homework? Maybe you don't want to seem nerdy or hurt her feelings. Or maybe you just want to see her do well. But consider that you worked hard on the assignment, and it's simply unfair for her not to put in the same amount of effort. If you give in, you'll feel taken advantage of. So give her an honest answer: say, "I'm not comfortable doing that," or "That's not such a good idea." You may want to soften the "no" by offering to help her with the assignment if she can get an extension. Your friend might be a little angry or become embarrassed because you challenged her. But if she's a true friend, she'll eventually see your point and respect it.

"I didn't study very hard."

Homework and tests are supposed to show the teacher what you know. If she thinks you understand, she moves on. It might sound clichéd, but you really are cheating yourself when you cheat. And there might be more to it than that. Do you doubt that you can get a good grade all on your own? Are you used to getting a lot of help on homework, or do you have trouble deciding when to turn off the TV and study? If you give yourself enough time to prepare and put in enough effort, you should have the confidence to leave the cheat sheet at home.

Caught?

It's likely to happen. And it's humiliating. What's the best thing to do?

★ Admit it.

★ Don't make excuses or blame others.

★ Accept the consequences.

★ Learn from the experience.

You'll save face and—most important—start to regain your teacher's trust.

friends

Dear American Girl,
Next year I am going to middle school. I am afraid I will lose my two best friends and I don't want to. What should I do?

Friends Till the End

In elementary school, your friends were probably the girls in your class or the girls in your neighborhood. You were with them the most often, and it was convenient.

In middle school, your old friends may still be your best friends. But you will also have the opportunity to find new friends who share your interests and make everything you do that much more fun.

The best friends for you are girls who

allow you to be yourself

and who

make you feel good about yourself.

They may or may not be the girls you played with in elementary school. In the end, your middle-school friends will likely be a blend of old and new friends.

friendless?

I just started middle school. The problem is that all my friends are going to a different school than I am. I really miss them. I know I'm going to make new friends, but how do I keep the old ones?

Alone

Just because you're going to a different school than your old friends doesn't mean you have to grow apart. Sure, you'll see each other a little less, but you can stay in touch day-to-day by e-mail, text, and phone. Think about throwing a back-to-school slumber party to talk about your different teachers, classes, and happenings. You could each invite a friend from your new school.

As the year kicks into full swing, you'll all be busier than ever. You may find it harder to touch base. But don't jump to conclusions when your friends don't return a call or e-mail you back right away.

In the meantime, spend your extra time getting to know other girls. That way, you'll be making new friends, and you'll still have the old ones, too.

Here are some ways you can let your old friends know they're still important to you:

★ Send a postcard out of the blue.

★ Remember birthdays.

★ Make a playlist of favorite tunes.

★ Start a book club. Read the same books and get together twice a month or so to talk about them.

Help! I just got my schedule. None of my friends are in my classes. What do I do?

In a Class All By Myself

Don't fret. You may find that you actually do better in class without your best buddy there to distract you. Think about all the good things that will come with being in different classes:

★ You'll meet kids you probably wouldn't have met otherwise.

★ You can share what happened in your classes with your old friends when you meet for lunch.

★ You can introduce new friends to old friends, and you'll meet your friends' new friends, too!

fading friendships

I think I've outgrown my best friend. She just seems like a baby sometimes. I am making lots of other friends, but I don't want to hurt her feelings. She doesn't have any other friends, though.

Stuck

It's pretty clear by now that you'll be going through a lot of changes in middle school—both physical and emotional. And the same will go for your friends, too.

Since friendships are often based on having the same likes and activities, you may find your relationships strengthening or souring over anything from fashions and fads to whether or not to wear makeup and become boy crazy.

Try to talk to your friend when other people aren't around and when you have time to share your feelings and listen to hers. Tell her what you're thinking: "We've been friends since first grade, and I still want to be friends with you. But I want to spend time with new friends, too." If you really do care about her, invite her to join in with your new group sometimes.

If you're the one who feels like your friend is growing up too fast, stay true to yourself. Do what you feel ready for inside, not just what she's into. Everyone grows up at a different rate. And sometimes this means you'll have to grow apart.

Growing apart gracefully

Growing apart is so awkward that it's often not talked about between two friends. It happens quietly by way of unreturned phone calls, less-frequent visits to each other's houses, even outright snubbing. But subtle clues can leave you feeling rejected, guilty, or unsure of yourself. You're full of questions:

"Why is she doing this?"

"Does she still like me?"

Or, on the flip side,

"If I pretend we were never friends, will she just go away?"

When a friend decides to break off a friendship with you, it can be painful, but there's not much you can do about it except find new friends. Sit with some different girls you'd like to get to know better. In time, a new friend will become just as special to you as your old one was.

If you're the one moving on, be considerate. Even though you don't want to stay close friends, you don't need to hurt her any more than you already have. Don't cut your ties completely. You'll feel better about yourself if you are kind—and you may want her friendship back one day.

For now, just make sure you're moving on for the right reasons.

make new friends

Are you new here?

The good news is, in middle school almost everyone is new! Kids from different elementary schools and private schools and even those who have been homeschooled come together in middle school. Since being new is something you all have in common, making friends shouldn't be hard. Here are a few icebreakers to help you get started with a prospective new pal:

★ Smile.

★ Save her a seat.

★ Stop by her locker.

★ Say hi in the hall.

★ Choose her to be your partner in class.

★ Offer homework help.

★ Give congratulations for a job well done.

★ Introduce yourself: "My name is Allie. I'm from Parkside Elementary. What school did you go to?"

★ Ask a question: "Who do you have for science?"

★ Pay a compliment: "I like your backpack."

★ Chat about the new school: "Is middle school what you expected?"

You'll meet lots of different kids in middle school. Some of them will be open to making a new friend; some of them won't. If your smile is not returned or your invitation to sit together at lunch isn't accepted, don't sweat it or think you're not likable. It may mean that this girl isn't looking for a friend right now. Maybe she isn't the right fit for you anyway. Or maybe she's even more uneasy about this "making friends" thing than you are.

Remember: You have lots of choices when it comes to the company you keep. Be assured that there's a girl out there looking for a friend just like you.

To meet girls who share similar interests, join an after-school club or team. It's a great chance to get to know girls in a more relaxed setting—outside the classroom—and do something that you love. (You'll know right away that you have at least one thing in common with other girls in the group!)

join the crowd?

You want to fit in. But to do so, you may find yourself making decisions based on what everyone else thinks, says, and does—and not on what you think, say, or do. Hello, peer pressure.

Will you swim with the crowd or against it?

That's up to you. In fact, that's a decision you'll make over and over throughout middle school. Each time you decide, consider the advantages and disadvantages. Some positives outweigh the negatives. Some don't.

In middle school it suddenly might feel more comfortable to go with the flow. But don't lose sight of your interests, your goals, and who you are just to blend in. Stay true to yourself. In the end, you'll be glad you did.

tough times

Underneath a layer of sweetness, some girls can be downright mean. Glaring looks. Cruel jokes. Eye rolls. Conspiring texts. Hurtful gossip. The silent treatment. These are just a few of the ways that girls can and do hurt each other. And, believe it or not, they are forms of **bullying.**

Here's how to deal:

★ **Shrug it off.** Look bored, avoid eye contact, and think to yourself *Whatever* or *I don't care.*

★ Calmly and coolly **tell the bully to stop** what she's doing: "Stop glaring at me," or "I want you to stop telling everyone I'm a cheater. It's not true." You can offer an explanation, but be careful not to let the bully know that she's getting to you.

★ Just **walk away** without acknowledging the bully. If online or texting, type "gotta go" and log off. Don't respond to mean messages directed at you.

★ If it keeps happening, **tell someone**—a parent, counselor, administrator, or teacher.

★ Don't wait for a teacher to notice. Teasing can fly under a teacher's radar because the attacks are sly and silent. **It's not tattling** if you report this kind of behavior to an adult.

★ **Arm yourself with a comeback** that you're comfortable with, such as, "That wasn't very nice. How would you like it if I said that to you?" Be careful not to add fuel to the flame with a fiery response, though. That just sends a message to the bully that her needling is working.

There's this boy at school who won't leave me alone. He deliberately bumps into me in the halls. Mostly it's embarrassing, but sometimes it really hurts. I asked him to quit it, but that just made him do it more. What should I do?

Fed Up

You have a right to feel safe at school. If someone's doing or saying things that make you feel threatened or uncomfortable—a girl, a boy, or an adult—tell an adult. In fact, tell two adults: a counselor or a teacher, and your mom or dad. They will see to it that the bully understands that what he or she is doing is wrong and needs to stop.

Troubles?

It would be so easy to pretend troubles never existed, right? But that doesn't give you the chance to face your feelings about what's been happening. When you ignore negative emotions, they can sink deeper inside you and eat away at you. Instead, talk about those not-so-pleasant things that happen to you—maybe to a parent, a counselor, or even in a diary. Get those emotions out, and you'll begin to feel better.

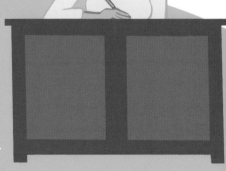

The School Counselor

What can she do? Lots! She'll

★ listen to your problem.

★ help you sort through your feelings.

★ explore ways to solve your problem.

★ help you decide what to do.

And what's more, you don't have to name names, and your conversation will be just between the two of you. If you need her help, sign up for a time to talk during a free period, at lunch, or before or after school.

the school dance

Middle-school dances are a lot like parties that you've gone to at friends' houses. You hang out, chat, giggle, snack on munchies, play music, and dance. The difference is you'll be doing all those things at school . . . in front of teachers . . . and all of your classmates. Anything can happen. You can make new friends. You can hang out with old friends. You can learn a new dance. A boy could ask you to slow dance. And, most important, you can have a great time!

Who's invited?

Schools hold dances to celebrate holidays or themes, to mark the end of a school year or the beginning of a new one, or just to give everyone a chance to get together. Dances are often open to all grades, but sometimes they are limited to just one grade. Some schools even invite students from all the other middle schools in the district. There may be a small charge to get in and a limited number of tickets, so be sure to buy a ticket in advance.

Get involved

Your school's student council or parent-teacher organization will most likely handle the details of putting on the dance, but they'll also need help from students like you. Think about volunteering to sell tickets, bring snacks or drinks, decorate before the dance, or clean up afterward.

Get ready

Decide what you will wear a few days ahead of time, and make sure it's clean. A casual dress or skirt may put you in the mood for a special night, but if you think you'll be doing some major dancing, your favorite jeans and comfy shoes might be a better choice. If you're not sure what to wear, ask some friends what their plans are. To help you sparkle under the dance lights, add something shimmery to your outfit.

The gang's all here

Get a group of friends to go to the dance together. There's safety in numbers, and you'll feel more comfortable walking in with your buddies. Once you're there, you can mingle and dance with other kids.

Dance basics

There's really no right or wrong way to dance. Before the big night, go online to learn popular dances. Practice your moves at home, and you'll be ready to hit the floor with confidence. It's all about moving with the music. For some people, dancing seems to come naturally, but for others, self-consciousness stops them from letting themselves go. When you venture out onto the dance floor, try not to worry about what others will think of you. Instead, sway your hips and move your arms to the beat. Once you've gotten into a basic groove, look around at how others are dancing. See if you can copy some of their moves. Group or line dances are also a low-stress way to get out on the dance floor.

Slow dancing

From time to time, the deejay at the dance will put on a slow song. Don't panic. If you're asked to dance (and you say yes!), you and your partner will put your arms loosely around each other and sway back and forth to the music. You may even chat while you dance in order to calm your nerves a little bit. (Psst . . . he'll have butterflies, too.) You can practice slow dancing at home with your dad, an older brother, or even your best friend.

If you don't pair up for a slow dance, take the opportunity to catch your breath. Head for the bathroom to freshen up, or grab a drink from the snack table. A fast tune will play again soon.

It's perfectly acceptable not to dance at all at a school dance. Lots of kids go for the food and fun but skip the fancy footwork altogether.

after school

Dear American Girl,
I just started middle school in a new town, and I don't know anyone! My mom said I should join a team, but I'm just not a sporty girl. What should I do?

Lonely

Everyone has a passion.

A *passion* is something that you have a MAJOR interest in. Something that you love to do no matter how much you do it. Something that makes you feel good about yourself when you're doing it. Something that you do well.

Middle school offers a wide range of after-school activities—more than just sports—to help you find or fine-tune your potential passions. Check out what's available at your school. By trying out different groups, you can try out all kinds of different interests (and people, too!). It's like tasting samples at the frozen yogurt shop before deciding which flavor to get.

My advice to girls starting middle school is to join a club. Get involved. Chances are, you will meet other girls who have the same interests.

what's YOUR passion?

Middle schools offer lots of clubs for you to join. Which one is right for you? To find out, circle all the things that you like to do.

★ Watch sports ★ Shoot hoops ★ Study the moon and stars ★ Kick a soccer ball around with friends ★ Keep your community green ★ Perform onstage ★ Do yoga ★ Speak in public ★ Explore local historical sites ★ Make an online scrapbook ★ Argue the pros and cons of a particular subject ★ Raise money for new school equipment ★ Design your own website ★ Make up dance routines ★ Learn to take better photos ★ Tutor younger kids ★ Do science experiments ★ Hit a home run ★ Write and recite poems ★ Play trivia games ★ Read to senior citizens ★ Sprint a mile ★ Visit kids in the hospital ★ Solve number puzzles ★ Swim relays ★ Spread the word about recycling ★ Jam in a band ★ Learn new gymnastics skills ★ Trade sitter secrets ★ Sing in a choir

★ Take care of animals ★ Chat about good books
★ Show your school spirit ★ Find out about
other cultures ★ Ride your bike ★ Compete in
a talent show ★ Create costumes for a play
★ Report the news by writing stories
★ Paint a mural ★ Ski the slopes
★ Make a scary movie ★ Make lunch
for the homeless ★ Cheer on your friends
★ Create crafts ★ Use strategies to
solve mysteries ★ Draw a cartoon

Count how many of each color you circled and write
the totals below.

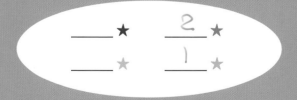

_____ ★   2 ★

_____ ★   1 ★

Now turn the page to find out what kind of club
might be right for you.

answers

★ mostly purple
Share your spirit

You've got the heart and determination to make a difference, so a **"get involved" club** is a natural choice for you. Whether you sign up to read to senior citizens or campaign for a safer school, your enthusiasm will spread easily to others and inspire them to join your cause.

Look into: Earth Club, Community Service Club, Student Council, Babysitting Club, Volunteer Club, Peer Tutors

★ mostly green
Sharpen your smarts

Looking to boost your brain power? An **academic club** will give you the challenge you seek. Field trips, guest speakers, and head-to-head competitions with other schools are just some of the perks you can look forward to.

Check out: Quiz Bowl, Math Olympiad, Science Fair, History Club, School Newspaper, Debate Team, Robotics Club, French Club, Destination Imagination, Model United Nations

★ mostly pink
Be creative

Explore your talents by joining an **arts club.** Whether you yearn to star in a play or sculpt with clay, you'll get insider tips and hands-on experience while perfecting your art.

Explore: Drama Club, Yearbook, Choral Group, Jazz Band, Art Club, Web Club, Crafts Club, Video Club

★ mostly orange

Get your game on

You're itching to move, so a **sports club** is definitely for you. Whether you try out for a competitive team or just play for fun with a recreational group, you'll learn new skills, do plenty of drills, and get lots of thrills. Be sure to listen to your coach—she'll help you become the best you can be.

Try: Basketball, Cheerleading, Pep Club, Soccer, Skateboard Club, Gymnastics, Softball, Cross-Country/Track

Need MORE reasons to sign up?

1. You can hang out with kids who share your passion.

2. You'll get to know kids from other grades and kids your own age whom you don't already know.

3. You can learn more about something you're interested in—without being tested on it!

4. You'll pick up expert advice from teachers and coaches.

5. You'll get great experience in a subject or sport that you like.

6. You can travel to other schools or visit cool places.

7. You'll gain experience working with a team or performing in front of others.

get psyched
for tryouts

Whether you're competing for a place on the team, trying out for the school play, or auditioning for chorus or band, preparation and having the right attitude can make all the difference.

Auditions

⭐ Find out all you can about the audition or tryout. Know when to arrive, what to bring, and where you will perform.

⭐ Ask the director or coach what skills he or she wants to see. Then set aside time each day to practice. Talk or sing in front of a mirror, or ask a friend to rehearse with you.

⭐ Get feedback from someone you trust. Say something like, "Don't just tell me I'm doing fine—tell me how I can do better!"

The night before the big day

Relax with your family or friends and get to bed early. Aim for at least ten hours of sleep. Try not to let bedtime turn into worry time—before going to sleep, imagine yourself performing perfectly. Just like on your first day of middle school, thinking positively will help make your dreams of success become real!

Calm, cool, and collected

Concentrate on the moment. Imagine a bird's-eye view of the tryout; then picture yourself close-up. Visualize yourself slicing through the water, delivering a great speech, or hitting every note. If you believe it, you'll achieve it!

Before you go on, take some belly breaths—inhale slowly from the bottom of your ribs, feeling the air fill your lungs. Exhale slowly and repeat. Try saying a calming word to yourself as you breathe, such as "Easy . . . easy . . . easy."

Fuel for thought

Snack on something healthy and hearty (an apple, cheese and crackers, or popcorn) about an hour before your tryout. To avoid dehydration, it's important to drink plenty of water before, during, and after a sports tryout. Of course, remember to take bathroom breaks, too!

Whoops!

If you make a mistake during your tryout, don't call attention to it. Just keep on going. Show your spirit and style by ending with a smile. Let the coach see you've got guts and determination—that's often what really counts!

chill out

Need more ways to calm your nerves and psych yourself up for tryouts? Try some of these ideas!

Pick a theme song. Choose something that makes you feel cool and confident or that motivates you. Play the song in your head whenever you start to get nervous.

Use good "scents." Experts say certain smells can affect your mood and energy. Try a lavender-scented lotion or bubble bath at night to help you relax. In the morning, a minty shampoo or shower gel will wake you up.

Find a thinking spot. Sit under a tree, hang out in your room, or go for a walk. Remember a time you felt great about yourself. Relive those moments for five minutes a day for several days before the tryout.

Dress for success. A week before your tryout, do a dress rehearsal. Make sure you have everything you need to wear or use and that it's all clean and in good condition.

Bring your lucky charm. As long as you've practiced faithfully, a lucky charm could give you an extra boost of confidence. If it's OK with your coach or director, bring one along.

My friend made the cheerleading squad but I didn't.
I'm feeling sad and left out. What should I do?

Cheerless

No question about it—not reaching your goal is tough. Don't give up,
though. If you tried out for something you love, stick with it. Ask the
coach for pointers so that you can do better next time. When you're
ready, think of some other way you could have fun this year. Then try it!

how much is too much?

On Mondays after school, I go to track and ballet, on Tuesdays I have ballet, on Wednesdays I have track and cheerleading, on Thursdays I sometimes have track meets, on Fridays I have Girl Scouts, on Saturdays I have swimming, and on Sundays I have church and cheerleading. I do so much, but I don't want to quit anything.

Busy Girl

Whoa! It might be time for you to take inventory of your personal time. There's a fine balance between being active and being overcommitted. Make sure you allow time for schoolwork, after-school activities, fun, and downtime. If a hectic schedule is what makes your internal clock tick, see to it that you stay super organized.

Schedule yourself

So much to do, but so little time to do it! Homework and after-school activities can take a big chunk out of your day. To make sure you have time for everything, turn to your planner or calendar.

Pick up where your school schedule leaves off, and plan what you have to do after school. Include club meetings, team practice, doctor's appointments, and, of course, homework.

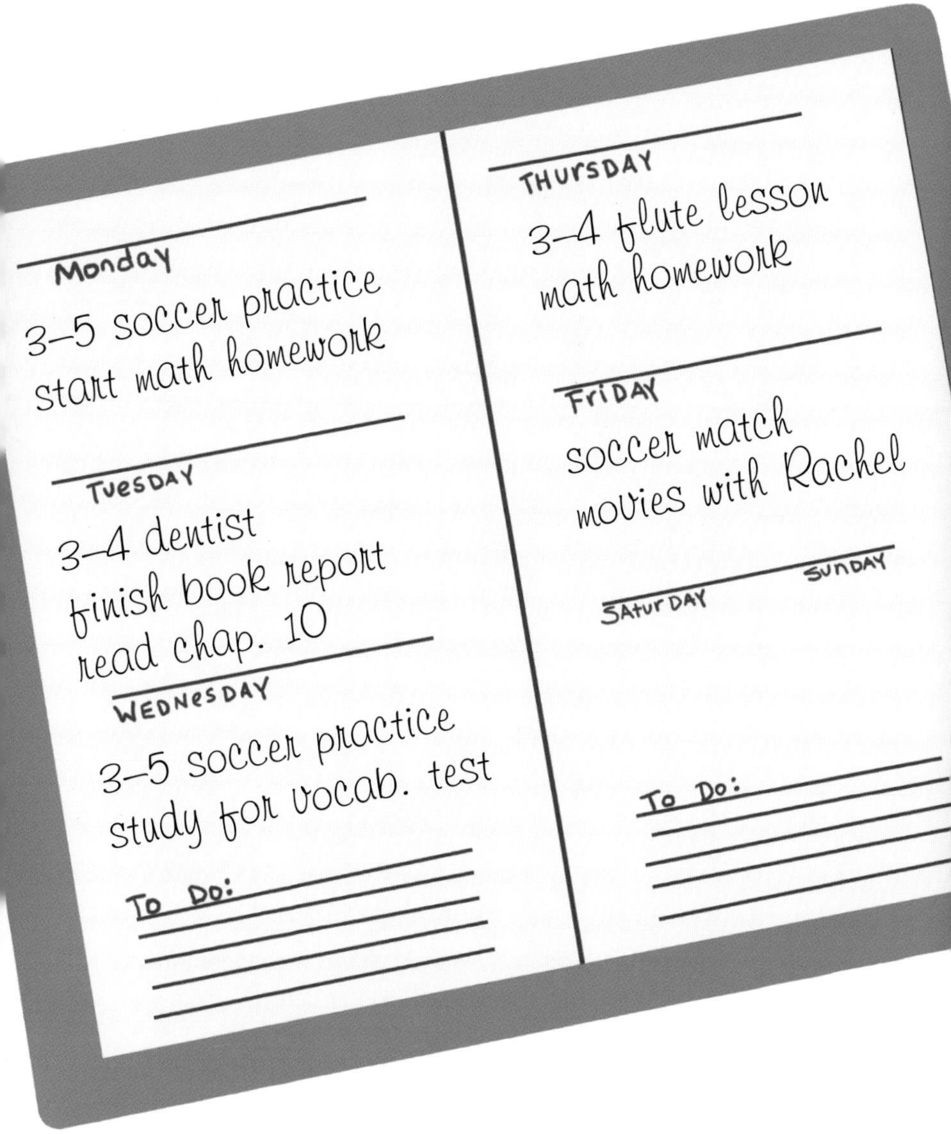

Monday
3–5 soccer practice
start math homework

TUESDAY
3–4 dentist
finish book report
read chap. 10

WEDNESDAY
3–5 soccer practice
study for vocab. test

To Do:

THURSDAY
3–4 flute lesson
math homework

FRIDAY
soccer match
movies with Rachel

SATURDAY   **SUNDAY**

To Do:

stressed out?

Everyone gets stressed out. It's a **completely natural reaction to change**—and you certainly have your share of changes when you start middle school. Anytime something happens to make you worried or afraid, your brain sends a signal to unleash a flood of hormones. These hormones race around your body creating all sorts of responses: Your heart beats faster, your breaths become shorter, your muscles tighten up, and your stomach shuts down. But you can stop those hormones from racing by playing some tricks with your mind.

Mind games

Don't mope! Try these ideas to cope with your worries.

Body melt

Find a quiet place to sit for a minute. Close your eyes or focus on a fixed object outside a window. Imagine that your feet are getting very, very heavy. Then your legs. Then your hands, arms, and shoulders, and finally your head. Reverse the melt by imagining your body gradually becoming lighter as the tension drains away.

Yell at yourself

Drive troublesome thoughts from your head. Next time you catch yourself feeling sorry for yourself, silently yell "Stop!" in your mind.

Huff & puff

Sit up straight, hold your shoulders back, and inhale deeply through your nose. Fill your lungs with as much air as they can hold. Then breathe out slowly and imagine your worries escaping into the air as you let go. Repeat as many times as it takes to drive the big bad wolf away.

Go on a mini vacation

Imagine yourself in a safe and relaxing place—the beach, the Eiffel Tower, or even your own bed. Use all of your senses to put yourself there—warm sand between your toes, the damp Paris fog clinging to your cheeks, the soft touch of your blanket. Snap out of it to find that you've become relaxed and refreshed.

Reality check

These tricks are only quick fixes to get you out of rough spots that come up at school and home. They may help calm the butterflies in your stomach for the moment. But if the butterflies keep coming back, it's a sign that you may need more help to deal with this problem. Talk to a parent or a school counselor to get the help you need.

More Stress Busters

★ Play a game.

★ Shoot baskets.

★ Kick a ball around the yard.

★ Hug a pet.

★ Take a walk.

★ Dance.

★ Talk to a sibling.

★ Call a friend.

★ Listen to music.

★ Do a puzzle.

commit or quit?

You'll be trying lots of new things in the next few years. Some activities will keep their sparkle and some won't. Should you stay or go? Ask yourself these important questions:

Why did I sign up or try out in the first place?

Was it what I dreamed of doing, or was it just a whim?

Did something happen to cause me to want to quit?

Is the activity something I still enjoy, or do I find myself dreading it?

Can I pick up the activity again later without losing out on too much?

Is it a temporary setback or a major turnoff?

What will I do with the extra time?

(Don't feel obligated to fill it)

Do I feel as strongly about the activity as I did when I started?

How to commit

With the extra time you'll have by giving up some other activities, you'll be able to focus on the ones that are most important to you.

Give yourself stepping-stones to a larger goal. Get tips from players on your team. Find a role model and read up on her. Talk with your coach or sponsor about how you can best help the team or challenge yourself more.

How to quit

Before making a decision to quit an activity, tell your parents what you're thinking. They may have some suggestions based on cost, your ability and level of interest, and your (and their!) time commitment for each activity.

Also consider the consequences of your decision. If you're on a team, other players or members may be counting on you. You might want to think about issues of timing or following through with a commitment, and either finish out a season or wait until after an important game or event to quit.

It's OK to give something up. But don't just stop going to practice and leave everyone guessing. Tell the club sponsor or team coach that you are quitting and explain why. Don't be ashamed or afraid. Your sponsor or coach may be sorry to see you go, but she won't be angry or upset at you. Say good-bye to other members and leave on a good note by saying "Have fun!" or "Good luck!"

"What do I do now?"

After you quit, you may feel a whole range of emotions—from relief to regret. You may relish the extra time you have to do other things but then find that you miss the team. Give yourself time to adjust to a new schedule. Stay in touch with old team or club members by asking them what the club is up to or cheering them on at games or meets. What you learned and experienced in the club or on the team will always stay with you. Just because you no longer belong doesn't mean you can't enjoy the activity from time to time.

you can do this!

Remember how you felt going off to school for the first time? Or how about your first day at gymnastics? Summer camp? Swimming lessons?

Think back to other times in your life when you successfully navigated a new situation. Then remind yourself, "Come to think of it, I CAN do this!"

Here's what girls said AFTER they started middle school:

Now that I am in middle school, I never want to miss a day of school. It's so much fun!

The best thing about starting middle school was all the new things: I've never had a foreign language class before, and I made new friends and joined new activities and clubs.

I think middle school is a whole lot more fun than elementary school. You're treated more like an adult.

I just started middle school. I love how I've made some incredible new friends, and I have some great teachers! You might think middle school is so scary—and so did I—until I tried it! I LOVE it!

Don't worry about going to the wrong classes. It happens to lots of people. The teachers are helpful and nice, and they'll direct you to the right place. Don't be nervous. Just concentrate on having a great day!

Just remember, you're not the only new kid. Every other person is new, too. Good luck!

How did it go?

Write to us and tell us about the highs—
and lows—of starting middle school.
What was easier than you expected?
What was harder? What do you know now
that you wish you'd known before?

Write to:

Middle School Editor
American Girl
8400 Fairway Place
Middleton, WI 53562

All comments and suggestions received
by American Girl may be used without
compensation or acknowledgment.
Sorry—photos can't be returned.